MARY CRATCHIT'S RECIPES

The Dickens' Village® Christmas Carol™ Cookbook

Published by
Neilan Lund
Heritage Yule Trim, Inc.

Editor—Judy Lund
Recipe Development—Diana Gulden
Design—Harry Hauck
Copy—Darleen Hauck
Illustration—John Stoneburg

ISBN 0-9649423-1-3

Printed in the United States
10 9 8 7 6 5 4 3 2 1
Second Printing

A Remarkable Discovery

Although it cannot be proven, it is believed that a packet of recipes recently discovered in The Old Curiosity Shop might have been recipes collected by Mary Cratchit.

This packet of recipes—tattered, torn and bound with old yarn—was found among stacks of papers and very old books. In the margins of these recipes were handwritten notes from conversations with Mrs. Fezziwig, Ebenezer Scrooge, Jacob Marley and others. While there is no proof, it is certainly possible that these were Mary's recipes. This surely was a remarkable discovery.

Many recipes in this book are adaptations from that very collection and are interpretations of food and festivities during the time of the famous holiday classic, *A Christmas Carol*, by Charles Dickens.

Contents

CHAPTER

1

Fezziwig's Christmas Eve Ball

Makes 8 servings.

Negus*

Potted Salmon*

Spiced Beef Brisket with Cumberland Sauce*

Assorted Breads and Rolls

Pickled Onions*

Mincemeat Pie with Hard Sauce*

Christmas Angel Trifle*

Recipe is included.

Fezziwig's Christmas Eve Ball was one of the
highlights every Christmas season. Mary Cratchit never
attended, but Mr. Scrooge would tell her about all the
festivities when he was an apprentice. The old warehouse
was cleared to make room for an abundance of good food
and an evening of dancing. All the lamps were lit and the
beams decorated with boughs, turning a workplace into a
warm, pine-scented ballroom.

Mr. and Mrs. Fezziwig with their three lovely daughters, other family members, friends and everyone employed in the business, arrived in their Christmas best to dance the night away.

The fiddler tuned up, couples bowed and curtsied, then "there were more dances, and there were forfeits, and more dances." Old Fezziwig was so quick on his feet "that he appeared to wink with his legs."

When the dancers gathered around the table, "there was a great piece of Cold Roast. . .and a great piece of Cold Boiled" with cake, negus and "plenty of beer."

Even young, shy Ebenezer Scrooge reveled in the excitement and gaiety of the Christmas Eve Ball. He had never seen old Fezziwig and Mrs. Fezziwig display so much delight while they watched their guests eat and dance throughout the festive evening.

Negus

a favourite drink served at English dances

750 ml bottle cold dry
   white wine or
   nonalcoholic white wine

Two 12-ounce cans cold
   lemon-lime beverage
1/8 teaspoon nutmeg

In a punch bowl or a large pitcher, mix all ingredients.
Serve in punch cups or small glasses.

Potted Salmon

Two 6-ounce cans skinless
   boneless pink salmon,
   well drained
6 tablespoons melted butter
2 tablespoons fresh lemon
   juice

Pinch of mace or nutmeg
Pinch of salt and pepper
1 tablespoon chopped
   parsley
Thinly sliced dark bread,
   cut into triangles

In a food processor or with a hand mixer, mix salmon,
butter, lemon juice, mace, salt and pepper until smooth.
Stir in parsley.

Pack mixture in a small bowl. Cover tightly with plastic
wrap. Refrigerate at least 6 hours or overnight. Remove
from refrigerator 1/2 hour before serving. Serve with
triangles of dark bread.

Spiced Beef Brisket with Cumberland Sauce

1 cup coarse sea salt
1 teaspoon allspice
1 teaspoon cloves
1 teaspoon mace
1 teaspoon nutmeg
1/2 teaspoon coarsely
  ground pepper

1/4 cup brown sugar
  (packed)
3- to 4-pound boneless
  beef brisket
1 cup chopped carrots
1 cup chopped onion

In a small bowl, mix salt, allspice, cloves, mace, nutmeg, pepper and brown sugar. Rub 1/4 of this mixture on both sides of beef brisket. Place in glass or ceramic dish. Cover tightly with plastic wrap. Refrigerate 24 hours.

Pour off liquid. Repeat procedure with remaining salt mixture for 3 more days. Carefully rinse brisket.

Fold brisket lengthwise in half and tie with kitchen string. Place brisket, carrots and onion in a large pot. Cover with cold water. Heat to boiling, then reduce heat to low. Cover and simmer about 3 hours or until brisket is tender.

Place brisket in a flat dish. Cover with a plate or small plastic cutting board weighted down with soups cans or other heavy object. Refrigerate at least 8 hours before serving. Cut into thin slices. Serve cold with Cumberland Sauce (below).

Cumberland Sauce

1 cup red currant jelly
½ cup port wine or grape juice

¼ cup orange juice
2 tablespoons lemon juice
1 teaspoon Dijon mustard

In a small saucepan, mix all ingredients with a whisk. Heat to boiling, then reduce heat to low. Simmer 5 minutes. Cool at least 1 hour before serving.

Note: If you wish, sauce can be made a day ahead and refrigerated.

This full-flavoured sauce is good company for cold meats and game pâtés.

Pickled Onions

2 cups distilled white
   vinegar
½ cup water
¼ cup sugar
1 tablespoon pickling spices

1 teaspoon mustard seeds
½ teaspoon salt
2 large white onions, cut
   into ¼-inch slices and
   separated into rings

In a large bowl, mix vinegar, water, sugar, pickling spices,
mustard seeds and salt, stirring until sugar is dissolved.
Stir in onion slices.

Cover with plastic wrap. Refrigerate 3 days, stirring
mixture occasionally. Drain liquid before serving.

*Historically, preserving food with vinegar or
salt gave some variety to winter meals when
fresh foods were not available. Today the
tangy flavor of pickled vegetables still
complements hearty meals.*

Mincemeat Pie with Hard Sauce

Favorite pastry for 9-inch
  two-crust pie
22-ounce can mincemeat
  pie filling

2 tablespoons coarsely
  chopped crystallized
  ginger (optional)
1 egg yolk
1 teaspoon water

Heat oven to 425°. Prepare your favorite pastry. Spoon
pie filling into bottom crust; sprinkle with ginger.
Cover with top crust. Trim excess pastry; seal edge with
a fork or decorative crimp. Prick top crust in several
places. Mix egg yolk and water; brush over pie.

Bake 10 minutes. Reduce oven temperature to 350°. Bake
25 to 35 minutes or until the crust is golden brown.
Cool slightly. Serve with Hard Sauce (below).

Hard Sauce

2/3 cup powdered sugar
1/2 cup soft unsalted butter

1 teaspoon rum or
1/2 teaspoon rum extract

In a small bowl, mix all ingredients until smooth.
Refrigerate, then remove 1 hour before serving.

Christmas Angel Trifle

Two 3-ounce packages
  cook and serve vanilla
  pudding and pie filling
7-inch round angel food
  cake (about 11 ounces)
2 tablespoons sherry

1 cup sliced strawberries
1 cup sliced kiwifruit
1 cup whipping cream
1 tablespoon powdered sugar
2 to 3 tablespoons toasted
  slivered almonds

Prepare pudding as package directs; cool. Cut cake into
2-inch cubes with a serrated knife. In a large glass bowl
or a trifle dish, place half of the cake cubes. Sprinkle
cake with 1 tablespoon sherry. Spoon half of the
pudding, then half of the strawberries and kiwifruit
evenly over cake. Repeat with remaining cake cubes,
sherry, pudding, strawberries and kiwifruit.

In a small bowl, beat whipping cream and powdered sugar
until stiff. Spread over fruit. Sprinkle with toasted
almonds. Cover with plastic wrap. Refrigerate up to
8 hours before serving.

Trifle, perhaps England's most beloved
dessert, combines cake and pudding in as
many ways as there are cooks. Add red
and green fruits for a festive Christmas
dessert that can be prepared ahead.

CHAPTER 2

Nephew Fred's Christmas Dinner
Makes 8 servings.

Mulled Wine* or Hot Apple Cider

Smoked Trout or Deviled Ham*

Roast Beef with Yorkshire Pudding*

Creamy Horseradish Sauce*

Roast Onions, Parsnips and Potatoes*

Brussels Sprouts with Crumb Topping*

Fruitcake or Syllabub*

Recipe is included.

N ephew Fred,
Ebenezer's sister's son,
was a cheerful,
handsome young man.
When he stopped at
Scrooge's Counting
House to wish his uncle
Merry Christmas,
Scrooge growled.

" 'Bah! Humbug!
Keep Christmas in your
own way, and let me
keep it in mine.' "

Fred invited his
uncle to dine with his
family, then continued
on his way keeping his
good spirit intact.

At home, Fred's lovely wife and her two sisters were busy with preparations for a traditional English dinner, Roast Beef with Yorkshire Pudding. As they worked, they talked about other Christmas dinners.

Fred joined them when he returned, remembering how his grandmother told of making Syllabub with fruit juice and warm milk straight from the cow, the streaming milk bubbling to a froth.

After dinner, everyone at Fred's house looked forward to music and singing and to playing games like Blindman's Buff, a wonderful excuse to be a child again.

Mulled Wine

warm and spicy, a drink just right for the season

750 ml bottle dry red wine
6 whole cloves
4 pieces of orange peel
   ½ inch wide

4 pieces of lemon peel
   ½ inch wide
1 cinnamon stick
1 tablespoon sugar

In a 3-quart nonaluminum saucepan, mix all ingredients.
Heat just to a simmer. Simmer 5 minutes. Strain to
remove spices before serving.

Deviled Ham

8-ounce piece of deli ham,
   cut into ½-inch cubes
3 tablespoons soft butter

2 teaspoons
   Worcestershire sauce
1 teaspoon Dijon mustard
   ⅛ teaspoon hot sauce

Place all ingredients in a work bowl of a food processor
fitted with the steel blade. Cover and process about
15 seconds or until smooth. Turn mixture into a small
serving bowl.

Cover tightly with plastic wrap. Refrigerate at least
4 hours. Sprinkle with chopped parsley if you like.
Serve with water biscuits.

Roast Beef with Yorkshire Pudding

4- to 6-pound beef rib eye
  roast
Coarsely ground pepper

Garlic salt
1/4 cup vegetable oil
Yorkshire Pudding (right)

Heat oven to 450°. Generously sprinkle beef roast with pepper and garlic salt; rub into roast. Place roast with the fat side up on rack in a roasting pan.

Roast 1 hour. Reduce oven temperature to 300°. Roast about 40 minutes or until a meat thermometer registers 140° for rare or 160° for medium.

About 10 minutes before roast is done, heat a 10-inch ovenproof skillet or a ring mold until hot. Pour vegetable oil into skillet. Prepare Yorkshire Pudding. Remove roast from oven. Cover loosely with aluminum foil. Immediately increase oven temperature to 450°. (Let roast stand 20 minutes before carving.)

While roast is standing, bake Yorkshire Pudding 20 minutes. Reduce oven temperature to 300°. Bake 5 to 10 minutes or until puffy and browned. (Carve roast while pudding is baking.) Serve pudding immediately.

Yorkshire Pudding

2 eggs   1 cup all-purpose flour
1 cup milk   ½ teaspoon salt

In a small bowl, mix eggs, milk, flour and salt until
smooth. Carefully pour over vegetable oil in skillet.

Creamy Horseradish Sauce

⅓ cup prepared horseradish
⅓ cup sour cream
1 tablespoon whipping cream

In a small bowl, mix all
ingredients until smooth.
Cover with plastic wrap.
Refrigerate at least 2 hours
before serving.

*Both Yorkshire Pudding
and Creamy Horseradish
Sauce are traditionally
served with the English
favourite, Roast Beef.*

Roast Onions, Parsnips and Potatoes

1 pound new potatoes
1 pound parsnips, peeled
  and cut into same-size
  chunks

8 small onions
¼ cup vegetable oil
Salt and pepper

Boil potatoes 5 minutes; drain. Mix potatoes, parsnips, onions and oil in 13x9-inch pan. Sprinkle with salt and pepper. Place in 450° oven with beef roast after roast has cooked 30 minutes.

Continue to cook in oven with roast, stirring occasionally, until vegetables are golden brown and tender. If roast is done before vegetables, cook vegetables until desired doneness either alone or in the oven with the Yorkshire Pudding. Cover with aluminum foil to keep warm until serving time.

Brussels Sprouts with Crumb Topping

Two 10-ounce packages
  frozen Brussels sprouts
1 ½ tablespoons butter

3 tablespoons dried bread
  crumbs

Cook Brussels sprouts as package directs; drain. Place in serving bowl. In a small skillet, heat butter over medium heat. Stir in bread crumbs. Continue stirring about 3 minutes or until crumbs are golden brown. Spoon over Brussels sprouts.

Syllabub

⅓ cup Madeira wine or
   apple juice

¼ cup fresh orange juice

¼ cup sugar

4 pieces of orange peel
   ½ inch wide

2 cups whipping cream

In a small bowl, mix Madeira, orange juice, sugar and orange peel, stirring until sugar is dissolved. Cover with plastic wrap. Refrigerate at least 2 hours or overnight.

At serving time, strain Madeira mixture into a large bowl. Add whipping cream. Beat with hand mixer on high speed until soft peaks form. Spoon into 8 stemmed goblets or dessert dishes. Serve immediately.

Syllabub stems from a bubbling
Elizabethan drink, originally clear
wine topped with a froth of cream.
Charles II was addicted to it for this
festive dessert is both elegant and fun.

CHAPTER 3

Cratchit's Christmas Dinner
Makes 8 servings.

*Roast Turkey with Sage and Onion Stuffing**

*Mashed Potatoes and Gravy**

*Sautéed Cabbage**

*Applesauce**

Peas

Bread

*Plum Pudding with Brandy Sauce**

Recipe is included.

Cratchit's Christmas Dinner was always a happy celebration. Preparation began weeks before when the family got together on Stir-Up Sunday, the Sunday before Advent. Each took a turn stirring the plum pudding to bring good luck during the coming year.

Christmas morning Mrs. Cratchit rose and "dressed out but poorly in a twice-turned gown, but brave in ribbons, which are cheap and make a goodly show for sixpence." Belinda, one of their daughters, helped with the table while Peter "plunged a fork into the saucepan of potatoes" and the younger children danced with excitement.

After dinner "Mrs. Cratchit entered: flushed, but smiling proudly: with the pudding, like a speckled cannon-ball, so hard and firm, blazing in half of half-a-quartern of ignited brandy, and bedight with Christmas holly stuck into the top."

Roast Turkey with Sage and Onion Stuffing

Sage and Onion Stuffing   12-pound turkey
  (page 30)   ¼ cup melted butter

Heat oven to 325°. Prepare Sage and Onion Stuffing.
Remove bag of giblets from turkey cavity; reserve giblets
for Gravy (page 32).

Rinse turkey thoroughly and pat dry with paper towels.
Spoon stuffing into turkey cavity (do not pack). Close
the opening with small metal skewers or trussing needle
and thread. Fill neck cavity with additional stuffing. Put
any remaining stuffing in ovenproof dish. Cover with
aluminum foil and refrigerate.

Place turkey, breast side up, on rack in roasting pan; brush
with butter. Roast uncovered 3 ½ to 4 hours, basting
occasionally with pan juices, until drumstick moves easily
and juices run clear when it is pierced with a fork.

Bake refrigerated stuffing covered during last hour of
roasting. Place turkey on heated platter. (Remove
skewers, if used.) Cover turkey loosely with aluminum
foil. Let rest 15 to 20 minutes before carving.

Sage and Onion Stuffing

3 stalks celery, chopped
1 large onion, chopped
1/4 cup butter
12-ounce package bread
   cubes
1 tablespoon rubbed dried
   sage leaves

1/2 teaspoon salt
1/4 teaspoon coarsely
   ground pepper
1 to 1 1/2 cups chicken
   broth

In a medium skillet, sauté celery and onion in butter until
tender. In a large bowl, toss vegetable mixture with
bread cubes and seasonings. Add enough chicken broth
to moisten mixture so it begins to stick together
(mixture should not be soggy).

Mashed Potatoes and Gravy

4 pounds baking potatoes,
   peeled and cubed
1 teaspoon salt

1 cup hot milk
½ cup soft butter
Salt and pepper

In a large pot, cover potatoes with cold water. Stir in the 1 teaspoon salt. Heat to boiling, then reduce heat to low. Simmer uncovered about 25 minutes or until potatoes are tender. Drain potatoes in colander, then return to pot. Shake over low heat briefly to remove excess moisture.

With a potato masher or an electric mixer, mash potatoes, gradually adding milk and butter until smooth. Season with salt and pepper. Serve with Gravy (page 32).

Gravy

3 tablespoons fat (from
    pan drippings)
5 tablespoons all-purpose
    flour

4 cups hot Giblet Broth
    (below) or chicken
    broth
Salt and pepper

Pour off all but 3 tablespoons fat from roasting pan.
Place roasting pan over medium heat. Stir in flour,
scraping brown bits from the bottom of pan. Cook and
stir 1 minute. Gradually whisk in Giblet Broth until
mixture is smooth. Heat to boiling, then reduce heat to
low. Simmer uncovered, stirring occasionally, about
10 minutes or until gravy thickens. Season with salt and
pepper. For a smooth gravy, strain before serving.

Giblet Broth

Turkey neck, gizzard and
    heart

6 cups water
1 teaspoon salt

In a medium saucepan, simmer all ingredients uncovered
1 hour.

Sautéed Cabbage

1 medium cabbage, cored
  and very thinly sliced
1 small onion, very thinly
  sliced

¼ cup butter
Salt and pepper

In a large skillet or Dutch oven, cook cabbage and onion
in butter over medium heat, stirring occasionally, about
20 minutes or until tender. Season with salt and pepper.

Applesauce

4 Granny Smith apples,
  peeled and cored
½ cup water

¼ cup brown sugar
  (packed)

Cut apples into 1-inch chunks. In a medium saucepan,
mix apples, water and brown sugar. Cover and simmer
over medium-low heat, stirring occasionally, about
20 minutes or until mixture is soft. Mash with spoon for
smoother texture, if you like.

Plum Pudding with Brandy Sauce

1 cup sultana raisins
1 cup pitted prunes, chopped
½ cup chopped candied fruit
¼ cup brandy or orange
   juice
1 cup sugar
½ cup soft butter
4 eggs
1 ½ cups fresh bread crumbs

½ cup all-purpose flour
½ teaspoon cinnamon
½ teaspoon ginger
¼ teaspoon nutmeg
⅛ teaspoon baking soda
½ cup chopped blanched
   almonds
Brandy Sauce (right)

In a medium glass or ceramic bowl, mix raisins, prunes, candied fruit and brandy. Cover and let set 6 to 24 hours.

Heat oven to 350°. In a large bowl, beat sugar and butter on medium speed until smooth. Beat in eggs until well blended. Mix in bread crumbs, flour, spices and baking soda with wooden spoon. Stir in fruit mixture and almonds.

Pour mixture into a buttered 1 ½-quart mold or soufflé dish. Place mold in baking dish or lasagna pan. Pour water into dish around mold. Bake about 1 hour or until golden brown. Serve warm or cool with Brandy Sauce.

Brandy Sauce

1 cup milk
2 tablespoons sugar
2 egg yolks
1 tablespoon brandy

In a small saucepan, heat
milk until bubbly around
edge. In a medium bowl,
beat sugar and egg yolks on
medium speed until thick
and creamy. Gradually beat
in milk on low speed.
Return mixture to small
saucepan. Cook, stirring
constantly, over *very low*
heat until mixture is thick
enough to coat the back of a
metal spoon. Remove from
heat. Whisk in brandy.
Serve warm.

CHAPTER
4

Tiny Tim's Caroling Party

Makes 8 servings.

Wassail, Apple Cider or Eggnog

*Cream of Stilton Soup**

*Oyster Stew**

Whole Grain Bread or Rolls

Bowl of Apples and Oranges

*Rice Pudding with Currants**

*Almond Shortbread**

*Roasted Chestnuts**

Recipe is included.

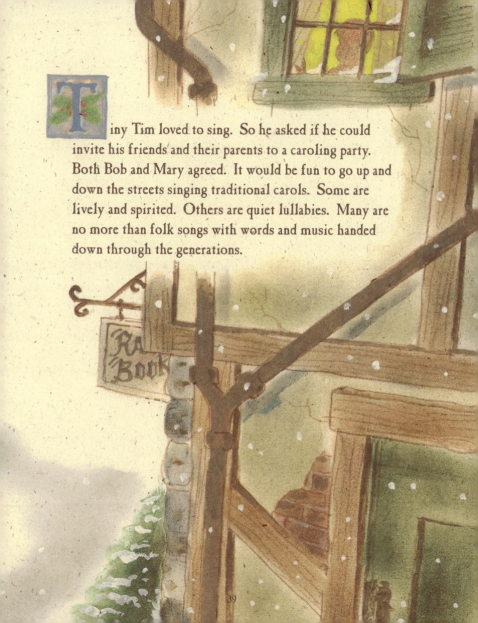

iny Tim loved to sing. So he asked if he could invite his friends and their parents to a caroling party. Both Bob and Mary agreed. It would be fun to go up and down the streets singing traditional carols. Some are lively and spirited. Others are quiet lullabies. Many are no more than folk songs with words and music handed down through the generations.

Tiny Tim and his mother planned a simple menu of hot soups, something hot to drink and something sweet. His brothers and sisters took turns carrying Tiny Tim to the homes of his friends to deliver invitations.

It was a night to look forward to, the fun of singing together, then sitting around a warm fire sharing stories and good, hot food.

The early Celts, the Romans, the French and even the Scandinavians all had traditions of merrymaking, singing and feasting when the winter sun was low in the sky. In the 19th century, the stories of Dickens helped to shape Christmas celebrations of joy and possibility.

Wassail

3/4 cup water

3 cups sugar

1 teaspoon freshly grated
   nutmeg

3/4 teaspoon ginger

3 whole cloves

2 allspice berries

1 cinnamon stick

750 ml bottle Madeira wine

1 cup brandy

In a 3-quart saucepan, heat water, sugar and spices to
boiling. Boil 5 minutes. Carefully strain spices from
syrup. Return syrup with Madeira to saucepan. Heat (do
not boil) about 5 minutes or until hot. Just before
serving, remove saucepan from stove and stir in brandy.

*Caroling and wassailing share a long history.
"Was hal" was an Anglo-Saxon toast to your
health. The first English carols were really old
wassailing songs. Today many people carry the
Christmas spirit from house to house, singing
carols and warming up with this hot, spicy drink.*

Cream of Stilton Soup

1 small onion, chopped

3 tablespoons butter

3 tablespoons all-purpose
flour

1 ½ cups milk

14 ½-ounce can chicken
broth

¼ pound Stilton cheese,
crumbled

Salt and pepper

In a medium saucepan, sauté onion in butter over medium heat until soft, but not browned. Stir in flour. Cook and stir about 1 minute or until mixture is bubbly and well mixed. Whisk in the milk and chicken broth. Heat to boiling, then reduce heat to low. Simmer, stirring occasionally, about 5 minutes or until hot and smooth. Turn off heat and stir in cheese until melted. Salt and pepper to taste.

Oyster Stew

1 pint shelled oysters
   with liquor
2 cups milk
1 cup whipping cream

½ teaspoon salt
4 to 6 drops hot sauce
Chopped parsley
Lemon wedges

In a medium saucepan, mix oysters, milk, whipping cream, salt and hot sauce. Cook over medium heat (do not boil), stirring frequently, about 30 minutes or until liquid is hot and oysters curl and float. Sprinkle with parsley and serve with lemon wedges.

Rice Pudding with Currants

4 cups milk
½ cup uncooked regular
   rice
½ cup sugar
½ cup currants
1 teaspoon vanilla extract
1 teaspoon finely shredded
   orange peel
Pinch of salt
Whipping cream

Heat oven to 300°. Mix all ingredients except whipping cream. Pour into a buttered 2-quart soufflé dish or casserole.

Bake uncovered, stirring occasionally, 2 hours. Continue to bake without stirring 20 to 30 minutes longer or until set and lightly browned. Serve warm. Pour whipping cream over each serving.

Almond Shortbread

1 cup soft butter
1/2 cup sugar
1 3/4 cups all-purpose
  flour

1/4 cup very finely chopped
  almonds
1 teaspoon almond extract
Pinch of salt

In a large bowl, beat butter and sugar on medium speed until smooth. Continue to beat in remaining ingredients until crumbly mixture gathers together.

Divide dough in half and shape each half into a ball. Flatten each ball on a parchment paper-lined cookie sheet into a 5-inch circle. (Circles should be at least 4 inches apart because dough will spread.) Prick circles randomly with a fork. Score top of each circle into 8 wedges with a knife (do not cut through dough). Refrigerate 20 minutes.

Heat oven to 325°. Bake 40 to 50 minutes or until lightly browned. Cut into wedges while warm.

Roasted Chestnuts

About 1 pound chestnuts

Heat oven to 425°. Cut an "X" with a sharp knife on the flat side of each chestnut shell. Place chestnuts in single layer in large pan. Roast uncovered 20 minutes or until shells begin to curl up at the "X." Peel chestnuts while they are warm.

"Carole" is an Old French word for a dancing song. Early carols were songs of celebration for any occasion. In the mid-1600s, Puritans stopped this joyful singing. But in the 1800's, Victorians brought carols back as part of the Christmas festivities.

After an evening of caroling, invite friends to sit around an open fire to roast chestnuts, hot and delicious.

CHAPTER
5

Young Marley's Boxing Day Breakfast
Makes 8 servings.

Winter Fruit Compote*

Poached Finnan Haddie*

Cheshire Scrambled Eggs with Mushrooms*

Bacon

Date-Walnut Bread*

Toast, Butter and Preserves

Baked Marmalade-Stuffed Apples*

*Recipe is included.

Young Marley so enjoyed inviting his family and friends to a Boxing Day breakfast. It was a leisurely morning to enjoy a special breakfast before going out to deliver boxes or gifts.

In England, this day after Christmas is a time to express appreciation to employees and others who supplied services throughout the past year.

Boxing Day originated with the traditional church alms-boxes opened for the poor on December 26th. Today, many give a Christmas bonus as a welcome thank-you to their employees for their services. And many continue to help the poor with a gift of their time or money to charity.

In the words of Marley's Ghost, "It is required of every man that the spirit within him should walk abroad among his fellow-men..." to see what could be "shared on earth, and turned to happiness!"

Winter Fruit Compote

1 pound assorted dried
    fruits (apricots, prunes,
    peaches, figs)

1 teaspoon sugar
1 cinnamon stick
Whipping cream or brandy

In a medium saucepan, cover fruit with water; add sugar
and cinnamon stick. Heat to boiling, then reduce heat to
low. Simmer about 20 minutes or until fruit is tender.
Serve warm (with or without the poaching liquid).
Drizzle each serving with whipping cream or a spoonful
of brandy.

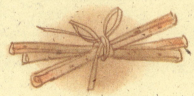

Poached Finnan Haddie

2 cups milk
2 cups water
½ teaspoon salt
⅛ teaspoon white pepper

2 to 2 ½ pounds finnan
  haddie, cut into 8 pieces
Melted butter
Chopped parsley
Lemon wedges

In a 12-inch skillet or Dutch oven, heat milk, water, salt and pepper to boiling, then reduce heat until mixture is barely simmering. Carefully place fish in skillet.

Cover and cook 10 to 15 minutes or until fish can be flaked with a fork. Cool a few minutes in poaching liquid. Remove fish with a slotted spoon to a heated platter. Generously drizzle with melted butter and sprinkle with parsley. Serve with lemon wedges.

Cheshire Scrambled Eggs with Mushrooms

Mushrooms (below)
12 eggs
1 teaspoon salt
1/8 teaspoon pepper

3 tablespoons butter
1/2 cup crumbled
  Cheshire cheese

Prepare Mushrooms; keep warm. In a large bowl, beat eggs, salt and pepper with a fork or wire whisk until mixture is well mixed. In a 12-inch nonstick skillet, melt butter over medium-low heat. Pour eggs into skillet, then stir the eggs gently as they begin to set. Sprinkle cheese over eggs, continuing to stir mixture until desired doneness. Spoon eggs onto heated serving platter; spoon mushrooms around eggs.

Mushrooms

2 tablespoons butter
1 pound mushrooms, sliced
2 lemon wedges

Salt and pepper
2 tablespoons chopped
  parsley

In a 12-inch nonstick skillet, heat butter over medium-high heat. Add mushrooms and sauté 8 to 10 minutes or until light golden brown. Squeeze lemon over mushrooms. Season with salt and pepper. Stir in chopped parsley.

Date-Walnut Bread

2 cups all-purpose flour
2 teaspoons baking
  powder
1/2 teaspoon salt
1 egg

1/2 cup brown sugar
  (packed)
1 cup milk
1/3 cup chopped dates
1/3 cup chopped walnuts

Heat oven to 350°. Grease and flour a 9x5-inch loaf pan.
In a small bowl, mix flour, baking powder and salt. In a
large bowl, beat egg and brown sugar with wooden spoon
until well mixed. Alternately stir in the flour mixture
and the milk until all ingredients are well mixed. Stir in
dates and walnuts. Pour batter into pan.

Bake 40 to 45 minutes or until golden brown and loaf
tests done (test with a toothpick). Cool completely
before slicing.

Baked Marmalade-Stuffed Apples

8 medium baking apples
½ to ¾ cup orange
   marmalade

4 tablespoons butter
Sour cream

Heat oven to 375°. Core the apples. Using a very sharp knife, make a very shallow cut through the skin all around the center of each apple. (This will prevent the apple from bursting during baking.)

Place apples in an ovenproof dish. Spoon marmalade into the core opening of each apple; dot each with butter. Bake 30 to 40 minutes, basting occasionally with pan juices, until apples are tender. Serve warm with a dollop of sour cream.

CHAPTER
6

Mary's Afternoon Tea

Makes 8 servings.

Darjeeling Tea with Milk

Earl Grey Tea with Lemon

Cucumber Sandwiches with Watercress Butter*

Open-Faced Smoked Salmon Sandwiches*

Herbed Egg Salad Sandwiches*

Scones* with Devonshire Cream and Strawberry Preserves

Chilled Lemon Sponge*

Spice Cake with Caramel Glaze*

Almond Macaroons*

*Recipe is included.

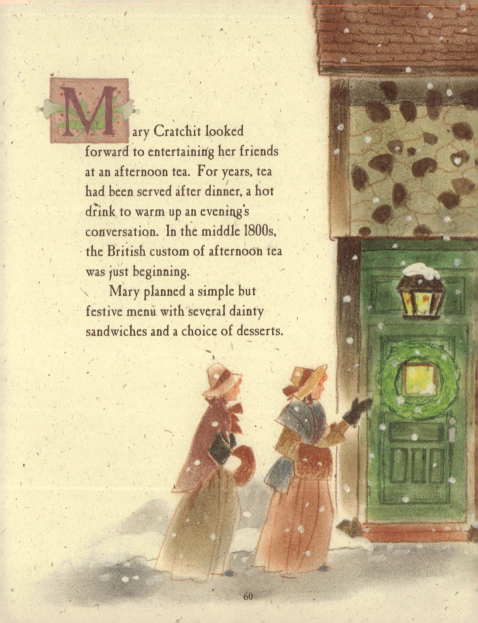

Mary Cratchit looked
forward to entertaining her friends
at an afternoon tea. For years, tea
had been served after dinner, a hot
drink to warm up an evening's
conversation. In the middle 1800s,
the British custom of afternoon tea
was just beginning.

Mary planned a simple but
festive menu with several dainty
sandwiches and a choice of desserts.

It was of upmost importance to make a proper cup of tea. Because it is again becoming a favorite drink, here are the secrets to a perfect cup of tea:

- Use cold water and bring it just to a boil.
- Warm the teapot with a swirl of boiling water.
- Pour this water out.
- Measure loose tea leaves, adding one teaspoon per cup and one for the pot.
- Pour boiling water over the tea.
- Steep for five minutes in a warm spot.
- Serve and enjoy a spot of tea.

Cucumber Sandwiches with Watercress Butter

¼ cup very finely chopped
    watercress leaves
¼ cup soft butter
½ teaspoon lemon juice
1 thin, firm cucumber,
    about 8 inches long

16 slices (about ⅛ inch
    thick) whole wheat
    bread
Salt and pepper
Watercress leaves

In a small bowl, mix chopped watercress, butter and
lemon juice. Cut the cucumber into very thin slices.
(A mandoline or food processor does this quickly.)

Spread a thin layer of watercress butter on each bread
slice. Arrange cucumber on 8 bread slices; sprinkle with
salt and pepper. Top with remaining 8 bread slices.

Carefully trim off crusts. Cut each sandwich into
4 triangles. Cover with plastic wrap and refrigerate until
serving. Garnish serving plate with watercress.

Open-Faced Smoked Salmon Sandwiches

¼ cup soft butter
2 tablespoons chopped
  fresh dill
½ teaspoon grated lemon
  peel
8 thin slices smoked
  salmon, about
  6x1 ½ inches

8 slices (about ⅛ inch
  thick) firm white
  bread
Chopped fresh dill
1 tablespoon tiny capers,
  drained
Lemon slices

In a small bowl, mix butter, chopped dill and lemon peel.
Cut each slice salmon crosswise in half.

Spread a thin layer of dill butter on each bread slice.
Arrange 2 slices of salmon on each bread slice.

Trim off crusts. Cut each slice diagonally into 2 pieces.
Sprinkle each with a little dill and a few capers. Cover
with plastic wrap and refrigerate until serving. Garnish
with lemon slices.

Herbed Egg Salad Sandwiches

6 hard-boiled eggs, very
   finely chopped
1/3 cup mayonnaise
1 teaspoon Herbes de
   Provence

Salt and pepper
1/4 cup soft butter
16 slices (about 1/8 inch
   thick) firm white bread

In a small bowl, mix eggs, mayonnaise and Herbes de
Provence. Season with salt and pepper.

Spread a thin layer of butter on each bread slice. Spread
egg salad on 8 bread slices. Top with remaining
8 bread slices.

Carefully trim off crusts. Cut each sandwich into
3 rectangular-shaped slices. Cover with plastic wrap and
refrigerate until serving

Note: A combination of 1/2 teaspoon dried thyme,
1/4 teaspoon dried basil and 1/4 teaspoon dried savory can
be used instead of the Herbes de Provence.

Scones

2 cups all-purpose flour	1 egg
2 teaspoons baking powder	1/3 cup plus 1 tablespoon milk
1 teaspoon sugar	Milk
1/2 teaspoon salt	Devonshire cream
5 tablespoons cold butter	Strawberry preserves

Heat oven to 425°. In a large bowl, mix flour, baking powder, sugar and salt. Work in butter with pastry cutter or 2 knives until well mixed and evenly crumbly. Mix in egg and the 1/3 cup plus 1 tablespoon milk to form a dough.

Knead dough on floured surface 1 minute. Roll into 7-inch circle. Cut into 8 wedges. Place on ungreased cookie sheet. Brush tops lightly with milk.

Bake about 15 minutes or until golden brown. Serve with Devonshire cream and strawberry preserves.

Note: A very fine quality cream cheese or unsweetened whipped cream can be used instead of the Devonshire cream.

Chilled Lemon Sponge

5 egg whites
Pinch of salt
Pinch of cream of tartar
1 ½ cups sugar
¼ cup soft butter
5 egg yolks
⅓ cup lemon juice

1 teaspoon grated lemon
   peel
½ cup all-purpose flour
1 cup milk
Whipped cream
Candied violets

Heat oven to 325°. Butter 2-quart soufflé dish. In a large
bowl, beat egg whites, salt and cream of tartar until stiff
peaks form. In another large bowl, beat sugar and butter
until well mixed. Beat in egg yolks, lemon juice and
lemon peel. Beat in flour, then milk. Gently fold into
beaten egg whites. Pour mixture into soufflé dish. Place
dish in pan of hot water.

Bake about 1 hour or until puffy and golden brown.
Cool slightly, then refrigerate until chilled. Serve in
dessert dishes or goblets. Garnish each with a dollop of
whipped cream topped with a candied violet.

Spice Cake with Caramel Glaze

2 cups all-purpose flour
2 teaspoons cinnamon
2 teaspoons ginger
1 teaspoon baking soda
½ teaspoon nutmeg
½ teaspoon salt

¼ teaspoon cloves
2 cups brown sugar (packed)
½ cup soft butter
2 eggs
8 ounces sour cream
Caramel Glaze (right)

Heat oven to 350°. Grease and flour a 9x2-inch round cake pan. Cut a piece of parchment paper or waxed paper to fit bottom of pan; grease paper. In a medium bowl, mix flour, cinnamon, ginger, baking soda, nutmeg, salt and cloves; set aside. In a large bowl, beat brown sugar and butter on medium speed until smooth. Beat in eggs. Alternately beat in some of the flour mixture and the sour cream until all ingredients are well mixed. Pour batter into pan.

Bake about 50 minutes or until cake tests done (test with a toothpick). Cool 10 minutes; remove cake from pan. Continue to cool completely on cake rack. Place cake on large serving plate. Pour warm Caramel Glaze over cake. Serve while glaze is warm.

Caramel Glaze

1 ½ cups brown sugar   ¾ cup milk
   (packed)   1 tablespoon butter

In a small saucepan, heat brown sugar and milk to boiling,
stirring constantly. Continue to cook without stirring
until mixture registers 235° (soft ball stage) on candy
thermometer. Remove from heat; stir in butter.

Cool mixture to 110°. Pour into small bowl. Beat on
high speed until thick and caramel colored.

Almond Macaroons

2 egg whites
Pinch of salt
Pinch of cream of tartar

8 ounces blanched
  almonds
1 cup sifted powdered
  sugar

Heat oven to 300°. Cover cookie sheet with parchment paper. In a large bowl, beat egg whites, salt and cream of tartar until stiff peaks form.

In a food processor, chop almonds very finely. In a small bowl, mix almonds and powdered sugar. Stir into egg whites until well mixed. Drop mixture by teaspoonfuls about 1 inch apart onto parchment-covered cookie sheet.

Bake 20 to 25 minutes or until light brown. Cool a few moments before removing from parchment paper.

CHAPTER

7

Scrooge's Twelfth Night Celebration

Makes 8 servings.

Claret Cup*

Roast Fresh Ham with Thyme*

Assorted Mustards

Scalloped Onions*

Pickled Baby Beets*

Celery Root Salad*

Apricot Fool*

Ginger Cookies*

*Recipe is included.

Scrooge opened
his home to the
whole neighborhood
for a Twelfth Night
Celebration. This
traditional end to the
Christmas season has
always been a time
for fun, games, plays,
merriment and all
sorts of revelry.

Twelfth Night
also marks the Feast
of the Epiphany
celebrating the
coming of the Magi
with their gifts of
gold, frankincense
and myrrh.

Now Christmas is drawn to a close. Scrooge is no longer "a squeezing, wrenching, grasping, scraping, clutching, covetous old sinner!" He has become a generous man.

"Scrooge was better than his word. He did it all, and infinitely more; and to Tiny Tim, who did NOT die, he was a second father. He became as good a friend, as good a master, and as good a man, as the good old city knew."

Claret Cup

Block or ring of ice
750 ml bottle dry red wine
Two 12-ounce cans
    gingerale

4 thin orange slices, cut
    in half

Place ice in punch bowl. Pour wine and gingerale into
punch bowl. Garnish with orange slices.

Roast Fresh Ham with Thyme

6-to 8-pound fresh ham
  (ask butcher to remove
  bone)

4 cloves garlic, chopped
1 bunch fresh thyme
Salt and pepper

Heat oven to 325°. Place garlic and thyme in bone cavity of ham. Sprinkle with salt and pepper. Roll up ham and tie securely with kitchen string. Place ham, fat side up, on rack in roasting pan.

Roast uncovered about 30 minutes per pound or until meat thermometer registers 170°. Remove ham to warm platter. Cover loosely with aluminum foil. Let rest 15 to 20 minutes before slicing.

Scalloped Onions

2 pounds boiling onions
    (about 1 ½ inches in
    diameter), peeled
½ teaspoon salt
2 tablespoons butter
1 tablespoon all-purpose flour

1 ½ cups milk
Pinch of nutmeg
Salt and pepper
½ cup finely shredded
    Gruyère cheese

Heat oven to 400°. In a large saucepan or Dutch oven, cover onions with water. Add the ½ teaspoon salt. Heat to boiling, then reduce heat to low. Simmer 10 to 15 minutes or until onions are just tender; drain.

In a medium saucepan, melt butter; stir in flour. Cook and stir 1 minute or until mixture is bubbly. Whisk in the milk, stirring constantly until mixture comes to a boil and thickens, then reduce heat. Stir in nutmeg. Season with salt and pepper.

Place onions in ovenproof casserole or dish. Pour sauce over onions and sprinkle cheese on top. Bake uncovered about 20 minutes or until hot and bubbly. Place under broiler 2 to 3 minutes to brown the top.

Pickled Baby Beets

Three 8 1/4-ounce cans
   whole small beets
1 small onion, thinly sliced

1 cup vinegar
1/2 cup water
1 cup sugar

Drain beets and reserve liquid. In a medium glass or ceramic bowl, place beets and onion.

Heat beet juice, vinegar, water and sugar to boiling. Boil until sugar is dissolved. Pour over beets and onion. Cover and refrigerate at least 8 hours.

Celery Root Salad

2 pounds celery root
2/3 cup vegetable oil
3 tablespoons vinegar
3 tablespoons Dijon mustard

Salt and pepper
3 tablespoons chopped
   parsley

Peel celery root. Cut with the julienne blade of a food processor. In a large glass or ceramic bowl, mix oil, vinegar and mustard. Season with salt and pepper. Stir in celery root and parsley. Cover and refrigerate 4 to 6 hours before serving.

Apricot Fool

1 pound dried apricots
2 cups white wine or water
2 tablespoons sugar
2 strips of lemon peel
1 cup whipping cream

In a large glass or ceramic bowl, soak apricots in wine about 6 hours or until well plumped.

In a medium saucepan, heat apricots, wine, sugar and lemon peel to boiling, then reduce heat to low. Simmer about 15 minutes or until apricots are very tender; drain. Rub the apricots through a sieve, or put through a food mill to puree. In a medium bowl, beat whipping cream on high speed until stiff; fold into apricot puree. Spoon into dessert dishes and chill until serving.

Ginger Cookies

2 cups all-purpose flour
1 teaspoon baking soda
1 1/2 teaspoons ginger
1/2 teaspoon cinnamon
1/2 teaspoon salt
1/4 teaspoon allspice

6 tablespoons soft butter
1 cup brown sugar
  (packed)
1 egg
1/4 cup molasses
Sugar

Heat oven to 350°. Cover a cookie sheet with parchment
paper. In a medium bowl, mix flour, baking soda, ginger,
cinnamon, salt and allspice. In a large bowl, mix butter
and brown sugar with spoon until well blended. Stir in
egg and molasses. Stir in flour mixture until well mixed.
Shape dough into 1-inch balls; roll in sugar.

Place balls 2 inches apart on parchment-covered cookie
sheet. Bake 10 to 12 minutes or until flat and crinkly.
Cool on a wire rack.

The Twelve Days of Christmas are a joyful celebration filled with food and festivities, caroling and wassailing, dancing and playing all sorts of games.

Then it is time to return to everyday life. Farmers once brought their ploughs to church to be blessed. The Bursar at Queen's College gives out needles threaded with coloured silk asking students to be thrifty.

Scrooge's promise echoes over the years, "I will honour Christmas in my heart, and try to keep it all the year."

Quotations in this book are from *A Christmas Carol* by Charles Dickens.

Index

A

B

Index

C

D

Index

E

Egg(s)
    salad sandwiches, herbed, 65
    scrambled, Cheshire, with mushrooms, 55

F

Finnan haddie, poached, 54
Fish
    poached finnan haddie, 54
Fruit
    apples, baked marmalade-stuffed, 57
    apricot fool, 81
    winter fruit compote, 53

G

Giblet broth, 32
Ginger cookies, 82
Gravy, 32

H

Ham, roast fresh, with thyme, 78
Hard sauce, 9
Horseradish sauce, creamy, 19

Index

Index

R

Index

The designs in this book are brought to life in Department 56, Inc.'s Dickens' Village® Series of handcrafted, lighted porcelain houses, buildings and coordinated accessories, sculpted from original drawings by master architect Neilan Lund.

For more information about The Dickens' Village® and the entire Heritage Village Collection® of fine quality porcelain collectibles, or to find the Department 56, Inc. authorized village dealer nearest you, contact:

ONE VILLAGE PLACE
6436 CITY WEST PARKWAY
EDEN PRAIRIE, MN 55344

1-800-LIT-TOWN